THE EXTERMINATOR

**A Play in Two Acts
by
Robert Alan Margolis**

Characters:

DAISY
A woman in her sixties.

HARRY
Daisy's husband. A man in his sixties or seventies.

BENJIE
Their son. In his twenties or thirties.

SAMANTHA
Benjie's wife. In her twenties or thirties.

THE EXTERMINATOR
A man in his sixties or seventies.

Setting

A house in the country. Stage Right is the living room. A section of the wall and ceiling has caved in, as if from an explosion. Water runs slowly into a large hole in the floor. There are two sofas, Stage and Upstage Right, a high-backed cushioned chair; a bar with assorted liquor and glasses. A stairway winds to an upstairs balcony, off of which are two bedroom doors. A number of dead cats hang in nooses from the living room ceiling. There are also empty nooses hanging. There is a pile of dead cats in the Upstage Right corner. Stage Left is the dining room, a large rectangular mahogany table and four high-backed chairs. The table is set for a party: Hats, favors, balloons, dishes, etc. Hanging from the rear wall is a large banner that reads: *Welcome Home Benjie*. A window sits beneath the banner. Stage Left has a doorway that leads to the kitchen and the out-of-view entrance. Upstage Left is a closet door. The house is in a state of meticulous decay. Even the rubble seems organized.

Time

The near future. Act I takes place in the afternoon. Act II takes place in the evening.

Note

If a balcony is not feasible, the bedrooms can be Upstage Right.

"To the future or to the past, to a time when thought is free, when men are different from one another and do not live alone — to a time when truth exists and what is done cannot be undone: From the age of uniformity, from the age of solitude, from the age of Big Brother, from the age of doublethink — greetings!"
- George Orwell, *1984*

"A screaming comes across the sky. It has happened before, but there is nothing to compare it to now."
-Thomas Pynchon, Gravity's Rainbow

The Exterminator
© Robert Margolis
Trade Edition, 2015
ISBN 978-1-63092-071-5

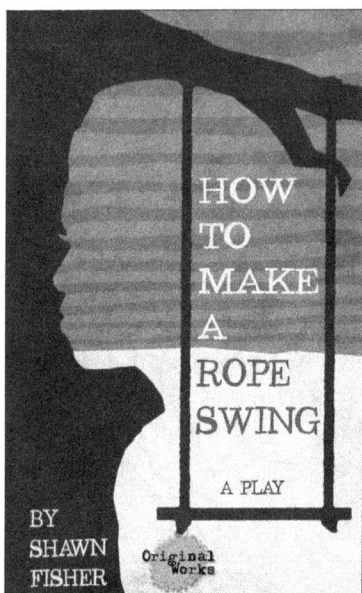

How to Make a Rope Swing
by Shawn Fisher

Synopsis: Delores Wright is the wealthy town matriarch and former elementary school principal and Bo Wells is the custodian who worked under her strict supervision for most of his life. When they find themselves stranded together in the old condemned schoolhouse, their reunion takes a dark turn and they relive their first meeting, decades earlier. It was 1952, when some schools were first integrated in this region nicknamed the "Mississippi of the North". Bo's wife, the school's first black teacher, was found drowned in a nearby river, hanging by her ankle from an old rope swing after it was rumored she had struck a white child. The papers dismissed it as an accident resulting from the "wild and drunken actions of a young colored woman". When Mrs. Wright reveals that she has dreams about the incident, Bo suspects she knows more than she admits. As the night grows colder and the failing health of Mrs. Wright becomes increasingly evident, Bo tries to understand his wife's final moments and Mrs. Wright's role in her death.

Cast Size: 1 Senior Male, 1 Senior Female, 1 Male (20s)

The Exterminator

ACT ONE

Scene 1

(AT RISE: Afternoon. DAISY is cleaning in the living room: Vacuuming, dusting, spraying, sweeping. She wears a dress, black shoes, and surgical gloves. HARRY enters from the kitchen. He wears a raincoat, hat, and boots. He walks, slightly stooped, with the help of a cane. He is carrying a dead cat by the scruff of the neck. DAISY ignores him and keeps cleaning. HARRY drags over a chair and hangs the cat from one of the empty ceiling nooses.)

HARRY: I found another one, poor little kitty.

DAISY: *(Still vacuuming.)* What was that?

HARRY: *(Raising his voice.)* I said I found him by the lake!

DAISY: *(Still vacuuming.)* You didn't go in, did you?

HARRY: Go in? Do I look like a complete idiot? *(DAISY keeps vacuuming.)* Do you think I've lost my mind? Well, I haven't. Not yet. Not by a long shot. I'm still on the ball. Still ticking. I can still see the forest from the trees. Don't forget who's who around this place! Do you hear me?! I'm talking to you! *(She continues to ignore him.)* What time's he coming?

DAISY: What's that?

HARRY: I said, when's he...

DAISY: *(Shouting.)* I've got a cake in the oven!

HARRY: Good.

DAISY: Chocolate.

HARRY: That's my favorite.

(DAISY stares at him.)

DAISY: You're dripping.

(HARRY looks down. He removes his rain gear. Underneath he wears a wet suit. Flippers hang from his belt. He removes this. Underneath the wet suit he is wearing Bermuda shorts, a bright Hawaiian shirt, black socks and sandals.)

HARRY: Not that I didn't want to go in. It looked so appetizing. To just dip my toe, for a second, would've been...

DAISY: Shut up, Louis! Will you please shut up! Stop blabbering and just settle down until I finish. I've heard enough out of you for one lifetime. Why don't you have a drink? You're all strung up.

HARRY: That's a good idea. I think I'll do just that.

(He goes to the bar and makes himself a drink. DAISY puts away the vacuum. HARRY sits in the large chair, sipping.)

HARRY: Who's Louis?

DAISY: What's that?

HARRY: I said who's Louis?

DAISY: Louis?

HARRY: Yeah. You called me Louis.

DAISY: Did I?

HARRY: Yeah.

DAISY: A friend. He…knew me…a long time ago.

HARRY: I don't remember him.

DAISY: *(Becomes caught up in the memory.)* I met him at a party, years ago. Too much to drink. Stumbling. I tried to stop him but someone had pulled the plug. Louis knew that. His hands wet, sticky. Each finger alert, almost knowledgeable. I cried out. My god, he was tall. His hands, aching, tried to move me. It was over too rapidly, even for someone as carefree as I was back then. But he held me tight, tight, my frail body gripping the air. Hand me that broom, will you?

HARRY: The name doesn't ring a bell.

(He hands her the broom.)

DAISY: Give me a hand with the couch.

(They move the Stage Right couch so DAISY can clean. They find a dead cat. DAISY picks it up and tosses it on the pile. She begins to sweep.)

HARRY: This sofa's a tough old bird. *(He strokes the couch tenderly.)* Good value. Last a lifetime. I remember this couch.

(He slowly looks up from the couch to where DAISY is bent over, cleaning. He creeps up behind her. He pinches her bottom.)

DAISY: Aaaah! What the hell...?

HARRY: C'mon Mary, and do your penance.

(He grabs her. He kisses her roughly. She tries to squirm free.)

DAISY: Get away from me you old sick bastard! Get your disgusting paws off me!

(HARRY tears open the front of her dress. DAISY shrieks.)

HARRY: Oh my! C'mon Mary...

DAISY: *(Interrupting.)* I'm not...

(She knees him in the groin.)

HARRY: Uhhh!

DAISY: ...your Mary. *(HARRY falls to his knees.)* You snake!

(HARRY glares up at her, his mouth open, breathing heavily. The doorbell rings.)

DAISY: Oh, god. He's here. *(HARRY doesn't move.)* Get up, you idiot!

(HARRY painfully tries to get up. He is too slow for her. DAISY grabs his arm and drags him violently behind the couch. They crouch there, hiding. The bell rings again.

*They don't respond. The bell rings twice more, rapidly.
There is the sound of an outside door opening & closing.
A dining room door squeaks slowly open. BENJIE sticks
his head in. DAISY simultaneously sneaks a look over the
couch. She remains watching throughout the following.)*

BENJIE: Hello? Anybody home? That's funny.

*(BENJIE places a suitcase and a duffel bag inside the din-
ing room. He is thin with close- cropped hair. He exits
briefly. He returns carrying SAMANTHA in his arms.
She is wearing a short skirt and black tights. She is holding a dead cat. BENJIE places her on the edge of the dining room table.)*

BENJIE : *(Whispering.)* There. Now it's official.

SAMANTHA: Not yet it isn't.

BENJIE: What do you mean? Oh.

(His eyes light up. He moves to her.)

SAMANTHA: Wait. *(He starts to kiss her.)* Oh, god.
    Wait.

*(He hikes up SAMANTHA's dress and climbs on the table
with her. She begins to unbuckle his pants.)*

SAMANTHA: Oh, don't. Not here.

BENJIE: Shhh!

*(They begin to make love on the table. BENJIE shoves all
the plates, party favors, etc. onto the floor to make room.)*

SAMANTHA: Oh, god.

BENJIE: Yes.

SAMANTHA: Oh.

BENJIE: Uh-huh.

SAMANTHA: Yeah.

BENJIE: Uh-huh. Uh-huh. That's it. That's...it.

SAMANTHA: Oh, oh, oh, yes.

BENJIE: Uh-huh. Uh-huh.

SAMANTHA: Yes.

BENJIE: Uh-huh.

SAMANTHA: Yes.

BENJIE: Uh-huh. That's right. That's...right!

SAMANTHA: *(Whispering.)* Tell me I'm a slut.

BENJIE: What?

SAMANTHA: Tell me...I'm a slut.

(The following is like a game they've played before, tenderly.)

BENJIE: You're a slut.

SAMANTHA: Tell me I'm a slut and a whore.

BENJIE: You are. You are.

SAMANTHA: Am I?

BENJIE: (*Tenderly.*) Yes. You're my slut. You're my whore.

SAMANTHA: Am I bad?

BENJIE: (*Tenderly.*) Very bad. Very, very bad.

SAMANTHA: Say it!

BENJIE: (*Whispering.*) Bad girl. Bad girl.

SAMANTHA: No. I'm not.

BENJIE: Yes. You're bad.

SAMANTHA: Noooo!

BENJIE: (*Whispering.*) Bad, bad, bad!

SAMANTHA: No, I'm not. I'm not bad. I'm not. Nooooh, god! I'm... Oh, god! Oh, god!!!

BENJIE: Yes...Yes!!

SAMANTHA: Oh, god! Oooooh!

(*She drops the cat.*)

BENJIE: Oh. Oh! Ooooh!! (*They both laugh. Breathing heavily.*) Well, how was that?

SAMANTHA: Now, it's official.

BENJIE: Good.

SAMANTHA: Help me up.

(*BENJIE gets up. He lifts her off the table. They adjust their clothing. They kiss. She lights a cigarette. A beat. HARRY emerges slowly from behind the couch. He stands there. BENJIE becomes aware of HARRY's presence. They stare at each other. BENJIE and HARRY edge warily towards each other. DAISY watches from behind the couch. When they get within a few feet of each other, they fall into wrestler's crouches and slowly circle each other for a few moments. Then they pounce. They grab each other's head and kiss intensely on the lips. They slowly slide to the ground while still kissing. When they reach the ground, they quickly break. Then they attack each other and start to wrestle violently. DAISY now jumps out from behind the couch, her fists and teeth clenched, shouting encouragement to HARRY. SAMANTHA leans calmly against the dining room table, smoking and watching.*)

DAISY: C'mon Harry. That's it! That's it!! C'mon, you old slug. Give it to him! Hit him where it hurts! Hit him where it... Goddamnit! Move your little lard ass. Kill him!! Kill the son of a...

(*BENJIE has forced HARRY onto the ground and is trying to pin him. DAISY drops to the floor next to HARRY and leans in, screaming in HARRY's face.*)

DAISY: C'mon, get up you old...You can do it! Don't give up! Don't give...C'mon, Harry! Fight!! Fight!! C'mooooon!! You stupid old...

(*BENJIE pins HARRY and smacks his hand on the floor. DAISY simultaneously smacks her hand on the floor.*)

DAISY: Shit!!!

(*DAISY gets up in disgust and moves away. BENJIE lies there for a moment. Then slowly gets up and walks towards DAISY. HARRY sees this. He starts to get up and sneak towards BENJIE from behind. He rises up to pound on BENJIE with his cane. At the last moment BENJIE, without looking back, kicks HARRY sharply in the groin. (HARRY doubles over onto his knees in pain.)*)

HARRY: Uhhh!

BENJIE: (*Gently.*) C'mon, dad. You always taught me to play by the rules, didn't you? Now fair is fair.

(*He slaps HARRY violently with the back of his hand. HARRY is knocked to the floor, unconscious. BENJIE now turns back to DAISY.*)

BENJIE: Hello, mother.

DAISY: Hello, Benjie. Welcome home.

(*He reaches out his hand. They shake hands formally.*)

BENJIE: Oh. I'm sorry. I haven't introduced you to my wife. This is Samantha.

DAISY: Your wife?

BENJIE: Yes. We're actually just newlyweds.

DAISY: (*Expressionless.*) Congratulations.

(*SAMANTHA walks over to DAISY.*)

SAMANTHA: It's a pleasure to meet you. Benjie has told me so much about you that I feel as if we're already aware of each other.

DAISY: Oh?

SAMANTHA: He told me that you kept the cleanest house in the neighborhood, that you were very thorough.

DAISY: Thank you, Benjie.

BENJIE: The place was always spotless. I can testify to that.

(*He raises his right hand as if being sworn in.*)

DAISY: I run a tight ship around here. There is no room for error in our continuing search for human perfection, especially during these unsettling times.

BENJIE: Why thank you, mother.

SAMANTHA: Oh, I just remembered. (*She goes and retrieves the dead cat she had arrived with.*) I found this outside. I didn't know...

DAISY: (*Interrupting.*) Just throw it on the pile. We've been having a small rodent problem lately. Somebody hasn't been doing their fair share in the war effort.

(*SAMANTHA hands the cat to DAISY. DAISY flings it violently against the wall and it falls onto the pile of cats.*)

DAISY: Somebody has been slacking off.

SAMANTHA: I've noticed that. The number of slackers has become quite evident in the major industrial zones.

DAISY: Is that so?

SAMANTHA: Yes. The uncleanliness is very distressing. And benign trauma medicine no longer seems to be doing the trick. (*DAISY snaps her fingers.*) That's it exactly! A little more discipline. A little more toe the line, and everyone would have enough food on the table.

(*During the preceding dialogue, BENJIE has gotten down on his hands and knees, looking for something while whistling.*)

DAISY: What's he doing?

SAMANTHA: Benjie, your mother would like to know what you're doing.

BENJIE: (*Looking under the sofa.*) I was just looking for Bootsie. Do you know where she's at? (*He looks up. DAISY doesn't answer.*) Have you seen Bootsie? I'm asking you a question. (*He goes right up to DAISY.*) Where the hell is Bootsie, you disgusting old sow?

(*DAISY stares at him and then marches to the cat pile. She shoves her arm into the center and pulls out a dead cat with a red bow around its neck. She brings it over and holds it out to BENJIE. He slowly takes BOOTSIE. He holds him with an outstretched hand, stares at him, and breaks down sobbing while he falls to his knees.*)

BENJIE: Somebody is going to pay for this. Somebody is going to die for this.

DAISY: (*Sharply.*) Benjamin! (*He looks up.*) Big boys do not cry.

BENJIE: (*Like a lost little boy.*) I'm sorry, mommy.

DAISY: We did not raise you to be a sniffler.

(*BENJIE wipes his eyes.*)

BENJIE: I'm sorry. I lost control.

DAISY: Well, don't.

BENJIE: It won't ever happen again.

DAISY: Good. Now get up and help me with your father.

(*DAISY takes Bootsie and hands it to SAMANTHA. DAISY and BENJIE drag HARRY to the couch.*)

SAMANTHA: Maybe we could have it stuffed. That's it. It could be cryogenically resurrected. I know a great place in the city that will have Bootsie looking better than new. It'll be just like your old companion again. Would you like that, Benjie?

(*SAMANTHA places Bootsie in their duffel bag. DAISY pulls a letter out from her dress.*)

DAISY: We've contacted all the appropriate authorities. They've stated in writing that a government employee will be coming by to determine the exact cause of the outbreak, that they've been made aware of the... (*She reads from the letter.*) "...accumulated seismic disequilibrium." We've been waiting for them.

(*DAISY exits to the kitchen. HARRY wakes up.*)

HARRY: Huh!

BENJIE: Hello, dad.

HARRY: Hello, son. Have you been here long?

BENJIE: Just a few minutes. I didn't want to wake you.

HARRY: That was very considerate. You're a considerate boy.

SAMANTHA: (*Reaching to shake HARRY's hand.*) Hello, I'm Samantha.

(*HARRY looks at her hand. He glares at her.*)

HARRY: The name doesn't ring a bell.

BENJIE: My wife, dad.

HARRY: Doesn't mean a goddamn thing to me, I said! You're barking up the wrong tree. (*He barks.*) Aarf! Aarf!

SAMANTHA: Meow!

HARRY: (*Giggling.*) That's my girl! (*HARRY takes her hand, sniffs it, and rubs it against his cheek.*) You've found yourself a real woman here. She's on the ball.

BENJIE: Of course she is, dad. She married me, didn't she?

HARRY: Well, I don't know about that. Will you be staying long?

SAMANTHA: Yes.

BENJIE: It all depends on conditions here, dad. It's a question of variety. I've been away for a long time. Now I'm back in the swing of things, looking for growth and successful business ventures, a little capital fixation to start out with, you know what I mean? (*He leans into HARRY and speaks with quiet intensity.*) You see I've been away for a long time, and now I'm back.

HARRY: Well, I'm sorry you won't be able to stay. Your mother will be very disappointed. It would've been nice to reminisce about the good old days.

SAMANTHA: Before the Release, you mean?

HARRY: I wasn't talking to you. I was talking to my son. Do you mind?

SAMANTHA: Before the onset of the Great Sickness. Is that the period you're referring to? Or are you talking about the War and its expected aftermath: Epidermal eruptions, reduced life expectancy, dementia, rapid increases in the malignancy-to-tumor household ratios?

HARRY: She's got a filthy mouth on her.

BENJIE: She's a historian, dad. And besides, I sense that she likes you. She feels she can open up to you. Reveal herself.

SAMANTHA: Peel off a few layers.

BENJIE: Become an intimate member of the family.

SAMANTHA: That's it! I really feel at home with you, Uncle Harry.

BENJIE: Then it's settled.

(*BENJIE goes to get his luggage. DAISY enters from the kitchen with cake and sparklers. There are shouts from BENJIE and SAMANTHA. Wild applause. DAISY carefully sets the cake down on the dining room table.*)

BENJIE: Bravo! Bravo!

DAISY: I made this from scratch as a festivity enhancer.

SAMANTHA: Splendid!

BENJIE: You've outdone yourself, mother! It looks magnificent.

(*BENJIE examines the cake. Scoops up some icing with his finger and brings it to his mouth enthusiastically while DAISY looks on expectantly. He stops. He sniffs it.*)

BENJIE: It's chocolate. (*He examines it carefully.*) It's chocolate, isn't it? I'm allergic to chocolate, don't you remember? It causes a wide variety of morbid symptoms in me. All of my orifices become inflamed. Ulcerated. I experience periods of depression, joint stiffness and penile arrhythmia. But you knew all that already, didn't you? Didn't you?! (*He moves menacingly towards DAISY. A beat.*) Yet still you found the time to make and bake it and for that I am eternally grateful. It gladdens my heart to see you so productive at such an advanced age, the little woman so nurturing and fecund under difficult conditions.

21

(*SAMANTHA sucks the chocolate off BENJIE's finger. BENJIE takes the luggage upstairs.*)

DAISY: (*Shouting.*) Wake up, Harry!

HARRY: Huh!

DAISY: Your son just gave me a compliment. You were too busy dribbling onto the couch to hear it so I thought I'd kill two birds with one stone. (*She holds a slice of cake out to HARRY.*) Do you want a slice of cake?

SAMANTHA: (*Taking the cake.*) Thank you.

(*DAISY glares at her. She cuts a slice for herself. They eat while HARRY stares hungrily.*)

SAMANTHA: It's delicious.

DAISY: You've known my son for a long time?

SAMANTHA: No. We just met.

DAISY: Is that so?

HARRY: Fly by night, eh? (*He flaps his arms.*) Caw! Caw!

SAMANTHA: (*Ignoring him.*): I'd never seen him before today, actually. His voice was familiar. But the details, the smell of his body, the protuberances, came as a complete surprise to me.

DAISY: I thought you were married.

SAMANTHA: Oh, we are. Husband and wife. A man-woman conglomerate.

HARRY: Where's your ring?

SAMANTHA: (*A beat. SAMANTHA turns slowly to him.*) What did you say?

DAISY: It's a simple question.

HARRY: Yes, it is.

DAISY: Shut up, Harry. So?

SAMANTHA: I lost it in the war. You have to understand. There were men everywhere, groping, touching, playing games with our frail bodies. We gave ourselves to them sometimes. A kind of penance.

(*BENJIE emerges from the bedroom and watches.*)

SAMANTHA: Like my father. Daddy. He used to touch me down there. His hands would explore the terrain. He'd move around, become knowledgeable. Mommy didn't know. She was asleep, she said. So daddy… touched. After that, I was numb down there for a long time. Oh, I could do it. I'd let men visit down there. I'd let them do me, play their pretend games. But I'd watch from the window: Touch and groan, touch and moan, touch and own, dry as a bone. Until Benjie. With Benjie, it was different. I met him at the supermarket. He brushed up against me as he walked by. It was electric. We talked. We went somewhere. I felt myself getting wet for the first time. Strange. Wet, down there. Ticking, down there. The movement of his body, tick-tock, tick-tock. My legs, my thighs, my own body touching his! I could feel that! A wall of glass had been removed. We were husband and wife. Our orgasms happened. Oh, god, it was glorious!

Then we dressed. We got in my car. We drove straight to your house. We arrived.

(*HARRY has fallen asleep. DAISY is expressionless.*)

DAISY: (*Moving rapidly to the kitchen.*) I'm so sorry you won't be able to stay. I'll just fix you something for your trip.

BENJIE: Please don't go to any trouble on our account, mother. We'll be using my old bedroom, of course. If you could just dust and scrub and fumigate in there, put on a clean supply of sheets and blankets, and remove all extraneous debris before nightfall, that would be great.

SAMANTHA: I'm a vegetarian, so all animal and dairy products will have to be expunged from the premises and the fridge will need to be sterilized. We can decide as a family what day would be most suitable for the group fast.

BENJIE: Samantha, why don't you give mother a hand with the kitchen reorganization.

SAMANTHA: Certainly.

(*SAMANTHA and DAISY exit to the kitchen. BENJIE watches HARRY sleeping. He walks over to him. Reaches out as if to touch his face gently. Stops. He carefully takes HARRY's cane, which he uses during the scene. He gently leans close to HARRY.*)

BENJIE: (*Shouting.*) Wake up!

HARRY: Huh!

BENJIE: (*Gently.*) Hello, dad.

HARRY: Hello, son. Have you been here long?

BENJIE: Just a few minutes. I didn't want to...

HARRY: (*Interrupting.*) That was very considerate!

BENJIE: Listen, dad. I thought we could have a man-to-man, shoot-the-shit, father-son thing to get reacquainted. You see... I've been away and now I'm back.

HARRY: (*Harshly.*) I'm busy right now. Don't bother me.

BENJIE: (*Like a child.*) I wonder if you could help me out, daddy. I need your advice on something that only a father would know. I think Samantha touched on it a little while ago, and I was hoping to ask you about it. (*HARRY starts to fall asleep.*) Ya see...Wake up!!

HARRY: (*Bolts awake.*) Huh!!

BENJIE: (*Like a child.*) Ya see, what I was wondering is this: When I was a little boy you used to come into my room at night. Do you remember, daddy? When you used to tuck me in? At night? In my old room? When you used to tuck me in, daddy? When you used to move your fingers along the sheets? In my room, daddy? (*HARRY nods off.*) Wake up!!

HARRY: Huh!!

BENJIE: When you used to squeeze me, daddy? Do you remember when you used to squeeze me? When your body would tremble against the sheets and your mouth would salivate inarticulate cries in the middle of the night, and you placed your body against my body in hard, pressing annihilation? Wake up!!

HARRY: Huh!!

BENJIE: When you used to initiate me, daddy, in secret ritual devices... (*Benjie imitates S.O.S. Morse code.*) ...signaling "deedeedeet-dee-deedeedeet. Deedeedeet-dee-deedeedeet?" When you did all that, daddy, would you label your behavior as: 1) an involuntary spasm? 2) a premeditated act of divine retribution? or 3) none of the above?

(*Silence*)

HARRY: (*Quietly.*) You ungrateful swine.

BENJIE: I was just curious, that's all.

HARRY: We should have aborted you when we had the chance.

BENJIE: Being away gave me a lot of time to think about all this.

HARRY: I disown you. You're disowned. I don't know you, you disturbed...

BENJIE: (*Interrupting.*) I just wanted to get the facts straight, daddy.

HARRY: They should have kept you up there for life. They should have put you to sleep like a diseased animal, like the cancerous mongrel that you are. They should have...

BENJIE: (*Interrupting.*) Because I'd like to accumulate some bedtime stories to tell my kids. Some real life adventure stories.

HARRY: Get out of here! Get out of my house you rancid piece of pockmarked vermin! Leave my house!

BENJIE: Because I'd like to set... (*BENJIE opens a switchblade to HARRY's throat.*) ...the record straight, daddy. *(He begins to unbutton HARRY's shirt.)* It's important to get the facts straight.

HARRY: (*Terrified.*) Nnnn...huh! Nnn...huh! Nnn...huh!

(BENJIE sings softly, as if to himself.)

BENJIE: "Don't be crucl...to a heart that's true."

HARRY: Oh, god. Oh, my god.

BENJIE: (*Whispering.*) Because I'd really like to know, daddy.

HARRY: My father....My father.

(HARRY faints. SAMANTHA sticks her head in from the kitchen.)

SAMANTHA: Am I interrupting?

(*BENJIE discretely puts away the knife and returns HARRY's cane.*)

BENJIE: No. We've just finished. Dad's napping.

SAMANTHA: Good. (*BENJIE sits lost in thought. SAMANTHA approaches.*) How are you?

BENJIE: I don't know.

SAMANTHA: Do you want to...

BENJIE: (*Interrupting.*) No. I don't know.

SAMANTHA: What's wrong?

BENJIE: Nothing.

SAMANTHA: You seem...

BENJIE: (*Sharply.*) What?! What do I seem?

SAMANTHA: I didn't mean anyth...

BENJIE: (*Interrupting.*) You didn't?

SAMANTHA: I just...

BENJIE: (*Interrupting.*) You didn't mean to...

SAMANTHA: (*Interrupting.*) No. I only wanted...

BENJIE: (*Interrupting.*) Why must you always inter-fere?! No one's asked for your opinion.

SAMANTHA: All right.

(A beat. SAMANTHA sits facing away from BENJIE. BENJIE sits facing HARRY. During BENJIE's speech, SAMANTHA slowly turns towards BENJIE. DAISY will enter from the kitchen.)

BENJIE: I'm sorry. I don't know what it is. Loose ends. Periods of putrefaction. *(A beat.)* I had a turtle, once. When I was little. We came home, found him belly up in the glass zoo. *(He laughs.)* I touched it. Sticky. Smelled of... I cried. *(He laughs.)* Can you imagine how ridiculous? Crying over a dead turtle.

(He is laughing hysterically. SAMANTHA comes over and touches his shoulder. BENJIE continues to face HARRY.)

BENJIE: Don't touch me.

(SAMANTHA rubs his shoulders tenderly. She kisses his head. BENJIE makes no effort to stop her.)

BENJIE: Please. Don't. *(She continues, tenderly.)* Don't do that. *(BENJIE is reliving something.)* Oh, god. Get the fuck off me. *(Quietly.)* Stop it. Please. Get your fucking hands off me.

(BENJIE has clenched his fists. His speech has shifted to HARRY, who remains sleeping. BENJIE is completely immersed in the memory.)

BENJIE: You prick. Don't touch me. Don't touch me you son of a bitch. Who the hell do you think you are? You son of a... Goddamn you...Goddamn you to hell! *(He gets down on his knees in front of HARRY.)* You son of a...Who the hell do you think you are? Wake up! Do you hear me! Wake up! You son of a bitch! Wake up! Wake up! Wake up!

(HARRY sleeps. SAMANTHA stands behind BENJIE, touching him gently. DAISY watches from the kitchen door. LIGHTS SLOWLY FADE.)

END OF ACT I, SCENE 1

ACT ONE

Scene 2

(AT RISE: *As soon as the lights have faded to black, they immediately come back on. It is a split second later. With the abrupt return of light, there is simultaneously an explosive Whoosh! and a massive cloud of white gas explodes into the house from the kitchen, bursts open the door, and obscures the entire downstairs. DAISY is knocked to the ground. As the gas begins to clear, we see that DAISY has crawled under the dining room table. SAMANTHA has dropped behind BENJIE, and has her arms wrapped around him. BENJIE kneels, his face pressed against HARRY's feet. HARRY continues to sleep, mouth ajar. At the doorway, a man has entered wearing a bright white asbestos suit with headgear. He carries a gun-like apparatus attached to a tank which is strapped to his back. He carries an attaché case. Cavalry music is playing loudly from a speaker on his belt. As he enters, he shoots occasional vapors from the gun. He shuts off the music. Everyone is choking.)*

EXTERMINATOR: Did somebody call the exterminator? We received word about a rodent problem in this sector. I was sent from the Ministry. Dispatched is probably a better word. Dispatched forthwith. I've got the documentation right here. *(He removes a form from his briefcase.)* Up to date. Correctly signed and sealed. Stamped. Passed through the hands of the proper authorities. Caressed. We're sparing no expense in our attempts to eradicate this sector's ongoing biological dilemma. We've got the manpower. We've got the credentials. And we're ready to kick some butt.

(He gives one final, sweeping squirt of his gun. He removes his gear. He is very well preserved. He has the look of a TV evangelist, a network news anchorman, and a hipster. He is wearing a zoot suit and tie. He is charismatic, charming and seductive: An "entertainer." He does a quick dance.)

EXTERMINATOR: We've tap-danced our way across hell just to be with you all today, folks. Is there a Daisy here?

(He sniffs around the room like an animal.)

EXTERMINATOR: C'mon now. Don't be shy. Here, Daisy. Heeere, Daisy.
(He sniffs something by the table. He smiles.) Fee, Fie, Foe, Fum, I smell the blood of...

(His arm abruptly shoots down and grabs DAISY's leg. He drags her out.)

EXTERMINATOR: Gotcha!

DAISY: Aaah!!

HARRY: Huh!

(HARRY wakes up and reflexively thrashes his cane through the air like a sword, above the heads of BENJIE and SAMANTHA.)

EXTERMINATOR: *(To DAISY.)* There you go. Good girl.

(He pats her on the head. He shows her the forms.)

EXTERMINATOR: Someone will have to sign these before I can start.

SAMANTHA: But you've already started, haven't you, without her signature. And now we've all been contaminated by that poison.

EXTERMINATOR: What? This spray? Only a harmless room freshener. Completely safe and natural.

BENJIE: Then why were you wearing that mask when you sprayed it?

EXTERMINATOR: You must be Benjamin. We've heard so much about you. It's a pleasure.

(*He holds out his hand. BENJIE refuses to shake.*)

EXTERMINATOR: You're the talk of the Ministry. Did you know that? A real success story. An honest-to-goodness Horatio Alger. When they first brought you in, you looked...Well, we've all seen the photographs.

SAMANTHA: I don't think...

EXTERMINATOR: (*Interrupting.*) We've met? No. Quite right. Samantha, isn't it? One of the memory people, I believe.

SAMANTHA: That's right. I'm a historian with the Office of Public Awareness and Accountability.

EXTERMINATOR: I know. I've read your work. A little unorthodox, but shows great promise. (*He clicks his heels.*) Enchanté, Mademoiselle.

(*He kisses her hand. Rubs his lips on it. SAMANTHA hesitates. Then slowly pulls away her hand.*)

SAMANTHA: That's Madame.

EXTERMINATOR: Oh?

BENJIE: We're newlyweds.

EXTERMINATOR: Really?

HARRY: There's no ring.

(*The EXTERMINATOR turns to HARRY.*)

EXTERMINATOR: Ah! The family patriarch. A great honor, sir. If you would kindly just sign this form, right...here, we can get started.

(*HARRY takes the form. Starts to read it.*)

HARRY: Wait a second...This says...I'm not signing anything until...

EXTERMINATOR: (*Interrupting.*) Sign it now, you incompetent old bag of wind!!

HARRY: (*Meekly.*) All right. (*He quickly signs.*) How's that?

EXTERMINATOR: (*Gently.*) Thank you so much.

(*The EXTERMINATOR puts away the form.*)

SAMANTHA: Have they determined what's causing the infestation?

EXTERMINATOR: Thank you for asking. We suspect it's the Jews, although our investigation is not complete. *(He snaps open his briefcase.)* As you all know, in the making of the Jewish Matz—Ah, *(He pulls out a slice of bright red matzah.)* ...the blood of Christian children is absolutely essential. We speculate that rodents and other sub-human, neo-hybrid life forms are being coopted by the Jewish race as an alternative source of spiritual plasma. The blood is drained from the bodies of the still-living creatures and siphoned into kosher glass vials that have been specially blessed by the Jewish rabies, their...religious leaders. What makes the situation all the more difficult is that Jews tend to reproduce at a feverish rate so that reliable information is very difficult to come by.

(He replaces the matzah in his case.)

BENJIE: I used to be a Jew.

DAISY: Benjamin!

BENJIE: I said used to be, that's all. I fell in with the wrong crowd for a while, in my youth. Don't you remember, mother?

DAISY: I have no idea what you're referring to.

BENJIE: Pieces of our past, linked together. Some stored chain of events. *(He begins to sing in Hebrew.)*:
"Boruch Ata Adonai,
Elohaynu melech haolam,
Asher kid'shanu b'mitzvotav…

(He hesitates, can't remember the last line)

BENJIE & SAMANTHA: (*Singing softly.*) Shel Ha...nu...kah. Ah...men.

(*BENJIE stares at SAMANTHA.*)

HARRY: (*To the EXTERMINATOR.*) I apologize for my son. He still suffers from occasional hallucinations.

EXTERMINATOR: Perfectly understandable. Relapses are not uncommon. After all, our rehabilitation procedures are still at the infant stage. (*The EXTERMINATOR rubs his eyes like an infant, crying.*) Wah! Wah!

HARRY: (*Giggling.*) That's very good!

(*The EXTERMINATOR moves to HARRY.*)

EXTERMINATOR: Goo-goo, gah-gah! Goo-goo, gah-gah!!

(*He sits on HARRY's lap and sucks HARRY's thumb.*)

HARRY: (*Beaming.*) That's my boy! He's an entertainer.

EXTERMINATOR: That's right! Very good. Very perceptive. (*He jumps up, grabbing HARRY's cane.*) So why don't you all sit back and enjoy the show.

(*DAISY tries to get up off the floor. HARRY falls asleep.*)

EXTERMINATOR: (To DAISY.) Allow me.

(*He takes her hand and gently lifts her up.*)

DAISY: (*Dazed.*) Thank you. I seem to...

EXTERMINATOR: ...have torn your dress. I see. (*He caresses the front of DAISY's dress.*) And such a beautiful dress. What a shame. It's all...torn up.

DAISY: My husband...

EXTERMINATOR: (*Interrupting.*) Don't worry. I think I have just what you need right here...Yes, indeedy.

(*He pulls out a needle and thread from his pocket.*)

DAISY: You've come equipped.

EXTERMINATOR: We aim to please. (*He begins to stitch her dress, tenderly.*) This little piggy went to market. And this little piggy stayed home. And this little piggy had roast beef. And this little piggy had none. And this little piggy went "wee wee wee wee wee", and couldn't find his way back home.

(*DAISY and THE EXTERMINATOR begin to kiss.*)

BENJIE: Mother!

(*HARRY wakes up and thrashes his arm through the air reflexively as if he has a sword.*)

HARRY: Huh! (*Realizes he doesn't have his cane.*) Where's my...? (*He sees them kissing. Stares.*) What's that? What's she doing? Where's my...? Give me my... What the hell is she doing?

(*The EXTERMINATOR stops. Turns to HARRY. A beat.*)

EXTERMINATOR: Goo-goo! Gah-gah!

(*A beat. Then HARRY giggles.*)

HARRY: Oh. It's a play. We're at the theater. (*He looks around. Then back to them, kissing.*) Atta boy! Give it to her! Give it...Oh my. Will you look at that? She's...Oh my.

(*HARRY laughs wildly. The EXTERMINATOR lifts DAISY up. Continues to kiss her as he carries her to the upstairs bedroom and closes the door. HARRY slowly forces himself to stand. He watches them leave. His face contorts, conflicted. A beat. He begins to applaud wildly.*)

HARRY: Bravo! Bravo! It's a happy ending. It's a...Encore! Encore! It's a...It's a... (*Slowly the smile leaves his face. He looks confused.*) Where's my cane? Where's my...?
(*He slumps back in his chair.*) Where's...?

(*He falls asleep. SAMANTHA leans against BENJIE, touching her dress. BENJIE leans against HARRY.*)

SAMANTHA: Do you want to play?

BENJIE: What do you mean?

(*She reaches to touch BENJIE's face.*)

SAMANTHA: Let's go swimming.

BENJIE: Swimming?

SAMANTHA: Let's go and take a dip. Just the two of us.

BENJIE: We didn't bring our suits.

SAMANTHA: We don't need suits. We're married now. We can go in as we are.

BENJIE: I don't know. I don't think it's safe.

SAMANTHA: Of course it is. It's very safe there by the lake. Calm. Stretches of sand. The water pressing against the shoreline, like fingers running along the beach. The sound of children, a rowboat moving up and down in the water. Our two bodies floating with the…

BENJIE: (*Interrupting.*) It's unclean.

SAMANTHA: No, it isn't. I've already...

BENJIE: (*Interrupting.*) It's diseased. There's something wrong down there. I'd meant to tell you sooner but otherwise engaged. Circumstantial evidence, I realize that. You deal with facts and figures. Dates of conquest. But this is a question of interpretation. Loose fitting garments. Medical examinations. It's called "Terminated Life Expectancy." The water filtered and re-filtered in every attempt to reconcile contradictory points of view. But someone was lying. That was understood. Someone had been altering documents. I should have spoken sooner, but now it seems...

(*They begin separately, but slowly come to face each other in a kind of ritual*)

SAMANTHA: (*Gently.*): Too late?

BENJIE: Yes.

SAMANTHA: Too late...

BENJIE: to speak out...

SAMANTHA: You want...

BENJIE: to question...

SAMANTHA: your sense of...

BENJIE: a kind of diminished responsibility.

SAMANTHA: The memory shield...

BENJIE: did much of it, it...

SAMANTHA: damaged me...

BENJIE: more than I could have...

SAMANTHA: understood.

BENJIE: Of course, I was...

SAMANTHA: young, then.

BENJIE: Yes.

SAMANTHA: Younger than...

BENJIE: God knew! He...

SAMANTHA: understood everything, he...

BENJIE: punished me over...

SAMANTHA: and over. I said

BENJIE: my god, my god, it hurts to...

SAMANTHA: touch you.

BENJIE: Reaching some...

SAMANTHA: barrier.

BENJIE: Yes.

SAMANTHA: Too many...

BENJIE: hurt fingers...

SAMANTHA: speaking incoherently.

BENJIE: Too many...

SAMANTHA: hurt fingers.

(*A longer beat*)

SAMANTHA: I'm going to go now.

BENJIE: All right.

SAMANTHA: To take a dip. I'll be back soon.

BENJIE: Of course.

SAMANTHA: Will you miss me?

BENJIE: Yes.

SAMANTHA: Good. (*A beat.*) Come here.

(*They hold each other. Kiss tenderly. SAMANTHA goes to leave.*)

BENJIE: Hurry back.

SAMANTHA: I will.

(*As she exits, SAMANTHA turns once to look at BENJIE. He is already looking away, lost in thought. SAMANTHA hesitates, then exits through the kitchen. A silence. The EXTERMINATOR emerges from the upstairs bedroom. He is tucking in his shirt and zipping up his pants.*)

EXTERMINATOR: Where's the little woman?

BENJIE: She's gone for a swim.

EXTERMINATOR: How refreshing.

BENJIE: I thought the water was...

EXTERMINATOR: (*Interrupting.*) Delightful! Magnificent! Pristine beauty!

BENJIE: I've heard otherwise.

EXTERMINATOR: Of course you have.

BENJIE: Unhealthy levels of...

EXTERMINATOR: (*Interrupting.*): Germ warfare! A thing of the past. This is the modern era. A land of technological miracles. Communism is dead, you know.

BENJIE: Fecal levels were reported to be...

EXTERMINATOR: (*Interrupting.*) Dirty jokes. Nothing more than...

BENJIE: (*Interrupting.*) Rashes. Hepatitis. Viral meningitis. Genetically altered limbs. Sea corpses. Splayed fingers and toes. Infants without mouths. Infants who...

EXTERMINATOR: (*Interrupting.*) Goo-goo! Gah-gah!

(*HARRY giggles in his sleep.*)

BENJIE: That doesn't work with me.

EXTERMINATOR: You're a very smart boy. Very gifted.

BENJIE: Who are you?

EXTERMINATOR: You've got a lot on the ball. You're...

BENJIE: (*Interrupting.*): What do you want?

(*The EXTERMINATOR slowly stoops over. He hobbles on HARRY's cane. He cups his ear. He begins to speak like an old man.*)

EXTERMINATOR: Eh? What's that, sonny? Could you speak up? (*He moves towards BENJIE, who stiffens.*) Will you give an old man a chance? Give an old man a place to rest his weary bones, would ya? (*He beckons with his finger.*) Come here, little boy.

(*BENJIE is frozen in place.*)

43

BENJIE: Go...away.

(*The EXTERMINATOR drops to the floor. He crawls and gropes towards BENJIE.*)

EXTERMINATOR: (*Pathetically*) Come on. Help me out. Please. You're so strong and I'm so tired.

(*BENJIE stands facing the audience, paralyzed, as if reliving something.*)

BENJIE: (*Quietly.*) Go away. Please.

EXTERMINATOR: You can help me, can't you? (*He rubs BENJIE's feet and legs.*) Goo-goo. Gah-gah.

(*HARRY giggles in his sleep.*)

BENJIE: Don't.

(*The EXTERMINATOR begins to move up BENJIE's body.*)

EXTERMINATOR: Give an old man a chance, will ya? (*He sings, softly.*) "Baby face, you've got the cutest little baby face."

BENJIE: (*Interrupting.*) Not now.

EXTERMINATOR: Yes, now.

BENJIE: Not this time.

EXTERMINATOR: So soft.

BENJIE: Don't.

(*He kisses Benjie's neck.*)

EXTERMINATOR: (*Tenderly.*) So very soft. Many gifted skin moments like yours.

(*The EXTERMINATOR puts his finger to BENJIE's lips.*)

EXTERMINATOR: (*Quietly.*) Don't tell. Please don't tell. A secret between me and you. Okay? Just me and you. (*He touches a tear on BENJIE's face. He tastes it.*)
   Tastes good, tastes sweet, these salty moments. Good boy. Good...boy. Now, you remember the hospital anthem, don't you? (*Singing.*) "It's about honor. It's about freedom. It's the courage to obey. We take our hand and make it..."

(*The EXTERMINATOR tries to move BENJIE's hand into a salute. BENJIE resists.*)

EXTERMINATOR: Wrong!

HARRY: (*Waking up.*) Huh!!

(*The EXTERMINATOR hits the back of BENJIE's knees so that he falls to the floor. HARRY watches. The EXTERMINATOR pulls BENJIE's arm behind his back.*)

EXTERMINATOR: Now let's try again, shall we?

(*He exerts pressure on BENJIE's arm.*)

BENJIE: Aaah!!

45

EXTERMINATOR: Sing.

BENJIE: I don't...Aaah!

EXTERMINATOR: Now.

(*HARRY begins to sing.*)

HARRY: It's about honor...

EXTERMINATOR: That's it. Hear that?

HARRY: It's about freedom...

EXTERMINATOR: (*To BENJIE.*) Go ahead.

BENJIE: (*Barks quietly.*) Aarf. Aarf.

EXTERMINATOR: That's it.

HARRY: It's the courage...

HARRY & EXTERMINATOR: (*Harmonizing.*) ...to
obey. We take our hand...
(*The EXTERMINATOR and HARRY both salute.*) ...
and make it sing, for a brighter day!

EXTERMINATOR: Got it now? Heh?!

BENJIE: (*Speaking.*) Make it sing...

HARRY: That's my boy!

EXTERMINATOR: Excellent.

BENJIE: It's about...

EXTERMINATOR: Yes?

BENJIE: It's about...

EXTERMINATOR: Good!

HARRY: Good boy!

BENJIE: We take our hand...

EXTERMINATOR: Yes!

HARRY: Goo-goo! Gah-gah!

BENJIE: Take it...

EXTERMINATOR: Our hand, yes?

BENJIE: Make it...

EXTERMINATOR: Sweetly, now.

BENJIE: Righteous...

EXTERMINATOR: Indignation!

HARRY: Guffaw! Guffaw!

BENJIE: Righteous, our...

EXTERMINATOR: Hands, yes!

BENJIE: Touching.

EXTERMINATOR: (*Singing.*) All those secret places!

(*BENJIE tries to crawl away.*)

BENJIE: All those attempted...

(*The EXTERMINATOR grabs BENJIE's legs and pulls him back. He climbs on top of him. DAISY emerges from the bedroom and watches.*)

EXTERMINATOR: Gotcha!

HARRY: All those hands!

BENJIE: All those...Wait!

EXTERMINATOR: All those...Go on.

BENJIE: Wait.

EXTERMINATOR: All those.

BENJIE: Aarf!

EXTERMINATOR: That's right.

HARRY: (*Howling.*) Ah-Oooooo!

BENJIE: (*Barking.*) Aarf. Aarf.

EXTERMINATOR: That's...it. That's...

BENJIE: (*Interrupting*) Not now. Please, not...

HARRY: Time's up. Time's up.

BENJIE: Not this.

HARRY & EXTERMINATOR: (*Howling.*) Ah-Ooooo!

BENJIE: Not this!

EXTERMINATOR: Tick-tock. Tick tick tick tick...

HARRY: Kaboom!

BENJIE: Not...

EXTERMINATOR: *(Interrupting.)* Tick tick tick tick...

HARRY: Kaboom!

EXTERMINATOR: *(Slowly.)* Tick...tick...tick...tick...

HARRY: Ker-Schplatt!!

(A long beat. HARRY and the EXTERMINATOR are breathing heavily and laughing. DAISY remains motionless, watching from the bedroom door. BENJIE slowly crawls out from under the EXTERMINATOR and moves to the dining room table. He looks up. He hesitates. He sees the cake on the table. He takes a scoop of chocolate cake icing. Tastes this. He voraciously eats the cake. He begins to break down.)

BENJIE: *(Starts quietly.)* Chocolate. Alkaloid drinking water. When I was a clown. Wanted to be. It had its charms. Or that time, dad, when we went to the circus. Red lights spinning in the black room, cracking against our face like egg. Or that time, holding hands. Candy cane and milk shakes. Sitting around the kitchen table, that sort of nonsense. Tick tick tick tick kaboom. Tick tick tick tick kaboom. Mesmerized, back then. *(A beat)* I stole things. Did you know that? Money, usually. Cans of soup. Sifting through the rubble, or else your worn-out grin, signal-

49

ing burnt flowers, bloated bellies of children, little corpses. You fucking... Deceit. Claimed never to have known, didn't you? Electrodes were applied. I remember now. The blinking lights consisted of men like yourselves. Even you, mother. Even you. Didn't want to assume responsibility. Turned your fucking heads. Stuck your fucking heads in chocolate gravy! Allergic. Allergic. Ka-choo! Gesundheit. Whooo-whooo! (*A beat. With quiet intensity.*) You filthy, stinking Jews. You...kikes. Shtinking juice. Gesundheit, shtinking, shtinking juice. Squeezed out...squeezed out...

(*BENJIE laughs. Pulls out his knife. He approaches the EXTERMINATOR, who is standing. He stands next to the EXTERMINATOR. BENJIE is gripping the knife, trembling, his hands clenching and unclenching.*)

BENJIE: All those rotten. Deceit. Deceit. (*He sings.*) "It's about honor. It's about freedom. It's the courage to obey. We take our...We take our..."

(*He drops to his knees in front of the EXTERMINATOR, who slowly salutes. HARRY salutes. DAISY salutes. BENJIE looks up. Rocking. A beat.*)

BENJIE: (*Quietly barking.*) Aarf. Aarf.

(*BLACKOUT*)

END OF ACT ONE

ACT TWO

Scene 1

(*AT RISE: Evening. Moonlight streams in from a hole in the ceiling. HARRY is asleep on the couch. We hear the sound of shoveling. We see dirt being tossed onto a mound from the hole in the floor, then the sound of a shovel striking a hard object. BENJIE emerges from the hole in the floor carrying an ancient dirt-encrusted suitcase. He is agitated, laughing and mumbling to himself as if being pursued. He sees HARRY sleeping. He moves towards him. Stops. Makes a decision. He moves quickly to the dining room table. He carefully brushes off the dirt and opens the suitcase. He removes a menorah and candles, places these on the table. He removes a prayer shawl and a black yarmulke, puts these on. He places the candles in the menorah. He lights a match, and smiles at the glow. He lights the candles while quietly singing "Little Boy Blue" and rocking back and forth.*)

BENJIE: "Little boy blue come blow your horn,
   The sheep are in the meadow/The cows are in the corn.
   Where is the little boy who looks after the sheep?
   He's under the haystack, fast asleep. Ah-men." Gesundheit.

(*BENJIE now begins to sing blues-style, as if in prayer, rocking back and forth. He reaches into his suitcase and pulls out an Old Testament bible. He begins to read.*)

BENJIE: "O house of Jacob, come ye and let us walk
   In the light of the Lord
   For thou hast forsaken thy people the house of Jacob;
   For they are replenished from the east

51

And with soothsayers like the Philistines
And they please themselves in the brood of aliens."

(*He laughs. He climbs onto the table. He begins to shift into a caricature of a preacher as he reads. DAISY emerges from the kitchen.*)

BENJIE: "And it shall come to pass, that
    Instead of sweet spices there shall be rottenness
    And instead of girdle, rags
    And instead of hair, baldness
    And instead of a stomacher, a girding of sackcloth
    Branding instead of beauty.
    Thy men shall fall by the sword
    And they mighty in the war
    And her gates shall lament and mourn
    And utterly bereft she shall sit upon the ground."
    Thus speaketh duh lawd!

(*He sees DAISY. He covers his face with one hand. Climbs down and hides under the table.*)

DAISY: What are you doing?

(*BENJIE pops out and bows.*)

BENJIE: Hail, Mary...

DAISY: (*With quiet fury.*) Benjamin.

BENJIE: Full of grace, our kingdom's...

DAISY: (*Interrupting.*) Benjamin!

(*He spits on the floor. Looks up.*)

BENJIE: Spittoon. (*Smiles. Shifts to British accent.*) "So brightly lit, isn't it? These fallow lands." That's a poem. Happy birthday, Auntie M. Come come come come come. Don't be shy.

(*He brings her to the table and seats her by the menorah. He hides under the table facing the audience.*)

DAISY: (*With controlled intensity.*) You mustn't indulge yourself like this, Benjamin. One mustn't give in to illness. We must be strong enough to...

BENJIE: (*Interrupting.*) Bare witness. Liquid testicles. Drip. Drip drip. Leaking again. Listen. Shhhh! Flames like tongues. Flames licking the air. (*He makes a slurping sound.*) Wheeeep! Rodents, auntie. Rodents speaking in tongues. Listen.

DAISY: You will be going back for some fine tuning. The doctor was very optimistic on the phone. He felt there was every possibility for a highly productive life if you could somehow maintain a kind of behavioral cleanliness. Keep yourself focused and on track.

BENJIE: (*Quietly, like a train.*) Whooo-ou-whoooo! Choo-choo-choo-choo, choo-choo-choo-choo, choo-choo-choo-choo, choo-choo-choo-choo...

DAISY: (*Overlapping with BENJIE'S train sounds.*) We were able to pull strings, Benjamin. We were lucky enough to secure you a berth aboard the "ship to psychic health and safety".

BENJIE: (*Quietly, while she speaks.*) I'm melting.

DAISY: They were very hopeful about...

BENJIE: (*Interrupting.*) I'm, I'm melting!

DAISY: (*Not looking at him.*) …about your future prospects. (*A beat.*) You threw away such great promise. Never fitting in. Always one step removed from normality. Even as an infant you seemed undisciplined. Chaotic. Soiling yourself at the most inopportune moments. Never able to follow the simplest commands.

BENJIE: (*Quietly*) Gesundheit.

DAISY: Now they have tests for this sort of thing. They've developed highly efficient ways of eliminating unwanted personality defects. Your disturbance could have been nipped in the bud. All of the distorted moments of childhood could have been eradicated, the gene pool made clean again through advanced sterilization procedures. You would have emerged a substance of immense worth and purity, an offspring to be proud of. (*A beat*) You were someone I once nourished. You were...

BENJIE: (*Whispering with quiet intensity.*) Eavesdropping.

DAISY: You heard...

(*They speak the following simultaneously*)

DAISY: … voices. You were too young to understand our concerns were always about the security of our nation and our allegiance to members of this household. We could not have known or understood what sick genetic landscape manufactured dirty secrets in your mind-craters whose government reports mentioned sound or touch factors involving electronic mind-silos hoping to regenerate the malformed nerve endings utilizing stimuli whose white benign metal frames the specialists called "reproductive apparatus" whose plans were never made clear to us, said "our mission" as we prayed for you, your hiding those fixed -grin skin eruptions as we all the time tried to correct the situation.

BENJIE: ... everything. Everything was considered too much to bear, wasn't it? Mutter und Fadder und diseased limbs pushed you away from my goal to never ever bleat-bleat deceive or else stuffed bodies in torn-out craters of these these these false messianic don't touch me! Your dreams were pillows then suffocating in electric houses where benign tumors touched your milk-white electronic reproductive apparatus devising plans which were never ever ready or "not our mission", our Jewish prayer shawls giving in to denial! while you hid your fixed-grin, endomorphic stupid hidebound eczema with all its holier-than-thou false promises, its filth-dreaming dried-skin simulcast always saying "no."

(*A beat. DAISY blows out the candles.*)

DAISY: We were never...

BENJIE: (*Interrupting.*) Lies!

DAISY: We were never...!

BENJIE: (*Covering his ears.*) Lies!!

DAISY: Now you are going to stop your nonsense right this second and listen to...!

(*BENJIE springs up and covers DAISY's mouth with his hand. DAISY struggles.*)

BENJIE: Shhh!

(*A beat. BENJIE hears noises in the kitchen. He stops. He throws DAISY over his shoulder and carries her down the bomb crater in the floor. The EXTERMINATOR enters from the kitchen carrying SAMANTHA, who is dazed and dripping wet. Her face and body are covered with boils, lesions and scars. The EXTERMINATOR wears a surgical mask and gloves. He lays her on the dining room table. He kisses her hand through his mask.*)

EXTERMINATOR: There you go. Feel better now?

SAMANTHA: (*Weakly.*) I don't understand. My skin...

EXTERMINATOR: Nothing to be concerned about. You just spent a little too much time out in the sun. You've gotten a slight burn, that's all.

SAMANTHA: (*Confused.*) A slight burn? But I...

(*The EXTERMINATOR pulls out a piece of chalk and begins diagramming rapidly on the wall.*)

EXTERMINATOR: (*Interrupting.*) Yes. You see the healing ozonic membrane has in effect symbiotically cathected the skin's pre-neuronal pathways causing a highly site-specific epidermal silence. Certain genetically gynecoid body parts moving in a reverse osmotic vacuum have responded with undue warmth and affection to the sun's overtures. Your skin has, in effect, become overly promiscuous with a concomitant loss of impulse control. Diagnostically speaking, we have before us a classic example of how premenstrual immorality can, when given enough of an incubation period, lead to advanced embryonic malapropisms. (*He points at her face.*) These lesions are indicative of the body's idiosyncratic guilt reaction to perceived misbehavior, a kind of masochistic billboard as expiation for severe bodily indiscretions. In other words, you are being punished for your sins.

SAMANTHA: (*Weakly.*) My sins? That's ridiculous. It was the lake water, not the...

EXTERMINATOR: (*Interrupting.*) Lake water?! (*He laughs.*) Delusions are unfortunately one of the many symptoms of the disease. I am highly optimistic, however, that with the proper treatment you will be able to attain to renewed health and vigor during a prolonged period of convalescence. Of course, there is always the danger of chronic sexual dysfunction with neuroses of this kind, so I believe that a thorough gynecological examination is called for. This shouldn't take long.

(*He pulls out a flashlight and begins to examine her.*)

EXTERMINATOR: Oh, yes. Oh, yes. The architectural complexity of the human organism is truly amazing. Let me see. Let me just...

SAMANTHA: (*Confused.*) Shouldn't there be a nurse in the room for this examination, doctor?

EXTERMINATOR: Does this hurt at all?

SAMANTHA: No. It feels...It feels...

EXTERMINATOR: Yes?

SAMANTHA: It feels...strange. What are you doing? I'm not...

EXTERMINATOR: (*Interrupting.*) It's all right. A nurse should be along at any moment to offer condolences. We're just going to perform a little advanced medical procedure to remove any blockages caused by the illness. If you'll just hold quite still, this will be over before you know it, before you can even blink an eye or wag a tail, an advanced medical tracheotomy will solve the problem. Very simply stated...

SAMANTHA: (*Interrupting.*) Wait a second. This isn't...

EXTERMINATOR: (*Interrupting.*) It's okay. I'm a surgeon. I've got many, many years of experience. I'm a licensed practitioner. I've been...Oh, yes I have...I've been...Oh, yes...

SAMANTHA: Nooo!

EXTERMINATOR: Oh, yes.

SAMANTHA: Stop it! Stop this! Help! Help!!

(*HARRY wakes up, whipping his cane through the air.*)

HARRY: Huh?! What? What's going on? I don't...

SAMANTHA: (*Interrupting*) Help me, Uncle Harry! Please help me! He's...

EXTERMINATOR: (*Trying to cover her mouth.*) Everything is under control, Harry. Everything is under complete...control. I'm...

SAMANTHA: (*Freeing her mouth.*) Uncle Harry, please help me! Stop him, he's...

(*The EXTERMINATOR again covers her mouth. HARRY staggers up and over to the table.*)

EXTERMINATOR: Go to sleep, Harry.

HARRY: Oh, no you don't. Oh, no you...

(*HARRY stops. Watches for a moment. Raises his cane as if to strike. Freezes. Then taps the EXTERMINATOR on the buttocks.*)

EXTERMINATOR: What is it? I've already told you...

HARRY: (*Interrupting.*) Hurry up, will ya? I'm next. I'm next in line. Hurry it up, goddamnit! I'm next in line. You've had your turn. Now it's my turn...Come on, now. Come on and let me! Come on.

(*Harry shoves the EXTERMINATOR and moves towards SAMANTHA.*)

EXTERMINATOR: Get off me, you buffoon!

(*He shoves HARRY to the floor. HARRY, stunned, watches.*)

HARRY: (*Begins to have a child's tantrum.*) Oh, my. Oh, my. It isn't fair! My turn! It's my...You can't do that! Can't do that!! You've had your...You've...

(*HARRY wraps his cane around the EXTERMINATOR and pulls him off. HARRY moves in. The EXTERMINA-TOR pulls HARRY off. They begin to struggle. The EX-*

TERMINATOR hits HARRY in the stomach. HARRY is thrown to the floor. The EXTERMINATOR moves back to the table. SAMANTHA is unconscious. HARRY watches, trembling and grimacing. He raises and lowers his cane.)

HARRY: It isn't right! It isn't... (*A memory begins to break through.*) My father. When I was little he used to... Pressurized cabins, that was it! Men in black uniforms. That was it! They held him down on the floor of the room. I watched them from the closet. His face, his eyes called out to me! He wouldn't confess. No. He was a stubborn bastard. The way he used to beat me. I didn't cry, though. Did not cry! They asked me. No, I said. A good man. He didn't even remember. Said said said nothing. Yes. He hurt me once. "Hurt, hurt, the empty gate. Hurt, hurt, the empty gate." (*He raises his cane. Inside a memory.*) You shouldn't have! Little boy watching you like that. You should stop that... (*He speaks in the caricatured voice of an old woman. Wags his finger.*) "Stop your nonsense this very minute! Do you hear me?! Stop that! What are you two doing in there? You come on outta there right this...Oh, my god! Oh, for heaven's sake."

(*The EXTERMINATOR has finished with SAMANTHA and sits in a kitchen chair facing the audience near HARRY. The EXTERMINATOR lights a cigarette. HARRY reaches to touch the EXTERMINATOR's leg.*)

HARRY: He wanted to say something special before they carried him off. I reached my hand to touch his good-bye Charlie face. His smashed in...Smashed in!! (*He lays his head on the EXTERMINATOR's leg, like a child. Speaks feebly.*) Now stop that. I said stop that, stop that, stop that. Please. Not right. Not right.

(He rubs his face on the EXTERMINATOR's leg. The EX-TERMINATOR and SAMANTHA lie still. BENJIE emerges from the hole in the floor. He is covered with dirt. He slowly walks to HARRY. DAISY's head pops up from the ground. BENJIE stands before HARRY and drops to his knees. He crosses himself and smiles.)

BENJIE: Forgive me father, for I have sinned.

DAISY: *(Calling out.)* He hurt me!

HARRY: *(Ignoring DAISY.)* What is it, boy? What have they done to you?

DAISY: Did you hear what I said, Harry? Your son hurt me.

HARRY: *(Tenderly touching BENJIE's hair.)* What have they done to my boy? *(Speaks to the EXTERMINA-TOR.)* What have you done to him?

DAISY: *(Advancing.)* He touched me. He wouldn't let me...

HARRY: *(Interrupting.)* He's not well. He's been...

BENJIE: *(Interrupting.)* Damaged by the war.

EXTERMINATOR: That's right.

DAISY: Don't be ridiculous.

BENJIE: Be meticulous.

DAISY: He's a danger to society. He's a danger to himself and others. He must be placed in a therapeutically -controlled environment. He mustn't be coddled like this.

HARRY: But they've done something to him! Can't you see that?! He's been unjustly accused. A man with a mask has attached electrodes to his private parts. He's my own flesh and blood. My own little boy. (*HARRY kneels and hugs BENJIE*) He's beautiful to look at, isn't he? He's a wee bit of heaven. He's a prince. Royalty! That's him. Look at him! Will you just...Why, he's...he's... (*A beat.*) He's the future!

(*DAISY, HARRY, and the EXTERMINATOR all turn and stare at BENJIE. A beat. HARRY raises his cane and slowly begins to beat BENJIE. DAISY waits, then attacks BENJIE also, kicking and beating him until he is unconscious. A beat. HARRY removes BENJIE's prayer shawl. The EXTERMINATOR carries BENJIE upstairs as HARRY and DAISY watch. A beat. HARRY then notices SAMANTHA. He looks closely at her. He leans over.*)

HARRY: (*Gently.*) Time to wake up, honey. C'mon, now. (*He gently shakes her.*) Time to get up.

SAMANTHA: (*Confused and weak.*) Oh, god. What? What is it?

HARRY: That's it. That's it. There you go. Nice and easy. (*He carefully helps her to sit up.*) Good girl.

DAISY: (*Softly.*) Miss?

HARRY: Excuse me, miss.

DAISY: You're on our table, miss.

HARRY: You're soiling our table.

(*SAMANTHA gets off the table and moves CENTER STAGE*)

SAMANTHA: I'm sorry. I seem to have...

DAISY: (*Interrupting.*) You've got a rash, miss.

HARRY: There's a stain on you. You're covered with some kind of a growth.

SAMANTHA: (*Dazed.*) I'm sorry. The lake. I went...

DAISY: (*Interrupting*) What's that? What did you say? You did what?

HARRY: Did you say "lake", miss?

DAISY: Of course she did. She's...

HARRY: (*Interrupting.*) Taken the plunge. Haven't you?

(*They begin to circle her.*)

DAISY: She's dripping. Look at her.

HARRY: She's a dirty, filthy manure pit. I could tell the moment I laid eyes on her. "Where's your ring?" I asked her. Do you remember? "Where's your ring?" I said. I knew even back then she was up to no good. And now we find out...

DAISY: (*Quietly.*) She's diseased.

HARRY: That's right.

DAISY: She's a carrier.

HARRY: Of course she is. But she's more than a carrier. She's infested.

DAISY: Oh god, no!

HARRY: Yes, she is. She's crawling with it. She's brought it into the house with her. You're virally degenerate. Aren't you, miss?

(*The EXTERMINATOR emerges from the bedroom.*)

SAMANTHA: I really don't understand what you're trying to...

DAISY: (*Interrupting.*) It's a simple question.

HARRY: Yes, it is.

SAMANTHA: This is ridiculous. I had no idea. It was only movement. A place of worship. A place of silence. To be apart from the crowds. The noise. Walking against the metallic screen images, flashing hand-held devices ticking away. Always waiting for some subtle vehicular nuance. Knives slashing the air. Sometimes groups of teenagers would set someone ablaze. You watched them roaming the streets, cans of gasoline, their faces all lit up by the flames. Alive pieces of dead machinery clogging the hallways. Everyone alive-dead, alive-dead. Tick tick tick tick kaboom. Tick tick tick tick kaboom. Women chased into empty lots, scarred, breathless, breathing the soot-blackened air. I've kept records of everything. I remember everything! (*A pause.*) I went in. Yes. I got wet. I admit it, all right. I did that. I'm guilty of that.

(*A beat.*)

DAISY: (*Gently.*) Of course you did. (*DAISY tenderly wraps the Jewish prayer shawl around SAMANTHA.*) It's all right, miss. You went in.

HARRY: You couldn't help yourself. You've been contaminated, that's all. What's done is done.

DAISY: It's not your fault.

EXTERMINATOR: Of course not.

(*DAISY and HARRY look at him. He begins to speak with the rhythms and cadences of an evangelist.*)

EXTERMINATOR: She's a victim of circumstances.

DAISY: You're just a victim of circumstances.

EXTERMINATOR: An orphan of history.

HARRY: Poor thing.

EXTERMINATOR: An empty vessel seeking its shore.

DAISY: Yes.

EXTERMINATOR: She's had a tragic existence.

DAISY: She certainly has.

EXTERMINATOR: And now she is...

DAISY & HARRY: Bereft of hope.

EXTERMINATOR: She's lost her sense of touch.

DAISY & HARRY: No.

EXTERMINATOR: She's lost her sense of smell.

DAISY & HARRY: Oh, my god.

EXTERMINATOR: She's lost the ability to enjoy the splendors of life on this planet.

DAISY & HARRY: Sigh.

EXTERMINATOR: And it isn't fair.

DAISY & HARRY: No?

EXTERMINATOR: It isn't right.

DAISY & HARRY: No!

EXTERMINATOR: It's an injustice!

DAISY & HARRY: That's it!

EXTERMINATOR: It's an injustice and a crime!

DAISY & HARRY: Of course it is.

EXTERMINATOR: And it mustn't be allowed to continue.

DAISY & HARRY: No.

EXTERMINATOR: She mustn't be allowed...

DAISY & HARRY: To suffer.

EXTERMINATOR: And there is a way.

DAISY & HARRY: Mmmmmm!

EXTERMINATOR: And is it humane?

DAISY & HARRY: Yes.

EXTERMINATOR: And is it merciful?!

DAISY & HARRY: Yes!

EXTERMINATOR: And is it gentle?!

DAISY & HARRY: Yes!

EXTERMINATOR: (*Quietly*) And what do we call it? We call it....

DAISY & HARRY: Euthanasia.

EXTERMINATOR: That's right.

DAISY & HARRY: Euthanasia.

EXTERMINATOR: Of course.

DAISY & HARRY: Euthanasia!

EXTERMINATOR: Good.

(*A beat. HARRY and DAISY get the broom and cane and move to SAMANTHA, who is lying down again and semi-conscious.*)

SAMANTHA: What? What is it? What do you want?

(*HARRY and DAISY raise the broom and cane as if to beat SAMANTHA but are stopped by the EXTERMINA-TOR, who raises his arms.*)

EXTERMINATOR: (*Like a minister.*) Please...approach.

DAISY & HARRY: Yes, doctor.

(*They approach the EXTERMINATOR. He hands them each masks and gloves as if at a religious ceremony. The ritual begins. They slowly put on the mask and gloves. They move to the closet and carry the EXTERMINATOR's spray device out to the couch. During this, the EXTERMINATOR clicks on his musical apparatus: Music from a string quartet begins to play. He begins to speak.*)

EXTERMINATOR: We save the souls of the sick. We save the souls of the dying. We save the souls of the genetically malformed. We save the souls of the librarians. We save the souls of the aged. We save the souls of the troubled minds.

(*HARRY and DAISY hesitate. Look to the EXTERMINATOR.*)

EXTERMINATOR: Please...proceed.

DAISY & HARRY: Yes, doctor.

(*HARRY and DAISY begin to place the mask on SAMANTHA's face.*)

SAMANTHA: Wait. Wait a second. No, no stop. Wait a second. No. Benjie? Benjie?! Benjie, please! Benjie!!

(*The EXTERMINATOR turns on the gas. He begins to read from BENJIE's bible as SAMANTHA dies.*)

EXTERMINATOR: "Whom have I in heaven but Thee
And beside Thee I desire none upon earth
My flesh and my heart faileth
But God is the lock of my heart and my portion for-
ever"
"For lo they that go far from Thee shall perish
Thou dust destroy all them that go awhoring from
Thee
But as for me, the nearness of God is my good
I have made the Lord God my refuge
That I may tell of all Thy works."

(*A long beat. DAISY sits facing away from everyone. HARRY slowly approaches the EXTERMINATOR who is seated facing the audience.*)

HARRY: (*Looking away.*) It's done.

EXTERMINATOR: Good.

HARRY: We've...done it.

EXTERMINATOR: (*Quietly.*) Good. Congratulations.

HARRY: (*Trembling.*) She's...

EXTERMINATOR: Yes?

HARRY: I don't know.

EXTERMINATOR: Of course not.

HARRY: I can't seem to remember. I used to, though. There are things I could tell you. It's done now, though. Isn't it?

EXTERMINATOR: Yes. It is.

HARRY: What's that? What's done?

EXTERMINATOR: You've completed the assigned task.

HARRY: I completed my assignment?

EXTERMINATOR: Yes.

HARRY: And did I do good?

EXTERMINATOR: Very good.

HARRY: Really?

EXTERMINATOR: Oh yes, indeedy. You were very impressive.

HARRY: Impressive? I was impressive?

(*The Exterminator beckons to HARRY.*)

EXTERMINATOR: Come here.

(*HARRY comes over timidly. He sits on the floor and places his head in the EXTERMINATOR's lap. The EX-TERMINATOR strokes HARRY's face.*)

EXTERMINATOR: That's it. Good boy.

HARRY: (*Like a little boy.*) I always wanted you to be proud of me. I thought about that a lot, you know. The times I wanted to hold you close. Your beautiful white body. You sang me to sleep. You did. (*A beat. HARRY sings softly, as if remembering.*) "Yie yieyieyieyieyie......." (*A beat.*) I love you.

EXTERMINATOR: (*Tenderly.*) And I love you, sweety. Now go and clean up your mess.

HARRY: My mess? I don't... (*HARRY sees the body.*) Oh. (A beat.) All right.

(*The EXTERMINATOR slaps HARRY hard across the face.*)

HARRY: Uh!!

EXTERMINATOR: (*Standing. Harshly.*) What's that? What did you say?

HARRY: (*Saluting.*) Yes...sir.

EXTERMINATOR: (*Gently.*) That's better. That's much better.

HARRY: Thank you, sir.

EXTERMINATOR: Good boy.

(*HARRY takes his cane and walks to the body. He turns to the EXTERMINATOR, who faces away from HARRY and towards the audience. HARRY hesitates, then takes hold of SAMANTHA's legs and slowly drags her body out through the kitchen while walking with his cane. A beat.*)

DAISY: (*Looking away.*) What's done is done.

EXTERMINATOR: That's an efficient way of looking at it.

(*DAISY looks over to the EXTERMINATOR.*)

DAISY: Thank you. That was kind of you to say. I've never really felt appreciated for my efficiency.

EXTERMINATOR: No?

DAISY: It's not something one is often praised for. I've always played by the rules, always maintained the discipline and coherence necessary for survival, but it seems to have gone unnoticed.

EXTERMINATOR: Really?

DAISY: Yes. It's as if there has always been a tear in my stocking, some small error that's come between myself and perfection.

EXTERMINATOR: You appear to be as nearly perfect a humanoid as one could expect during these chaotic times.

DAISY: That's sweet. You have a way with words. Did you know that?

EXTERMINATOR: Do I? (*He moves to the bar to mix them drinks.*) I was a writer once, before my most recent assignment.

DAISY: Oh, really? You wrote things down, then. You...kept lists?

EXTERMINATOR: Something like that. Yes. Words placed one against the other. The power of words to inspire, to move, to transform. I continue to find them very useful in my current line of work.

DAISY: I've noticed that. You have a way with people.

EXTERMINATOR: Thank you.

DAISY: Have you ever thought about running for higher office?

EXTERMINATOR: I've considered it, yes. There's been some enthusiasm for that idea at the Ministry, although I must admit that I like the freedom and flexibility of my current position. I'm not really a desk kind of person, if you follow my meaning.

DAISY: Yes.

(*He serves the drinks. They toast.*)

EXTERMINATOR: L'Chaim.

(*They drink.*)

DAISY: You're a religious person, then?

EXTERMINATOR: I like to think of myself as a secular humanist. I'm concerned with what's best for our society as a whole. "The best and the brightest". To my mind, sin is not a dilemma of ethics but a question of discipline. Too often what we've mistakenly labeled "Democracy" is, in fact, a kind of cultural thuggishness: A bunch of greedy, selfish children all clamoring for their own personal suck at the public teat. My hope, my dream is to elevate this great nation, to bring it back its sense of national pride, so that together as members of the same team we can once again unite as one body, one voice, in order to fully attain to our glorious heritage, our birthright!

(*DAISY applauds.*)

DAISY: That was very inspiring.

EXTERMINATOR: I apologize for my...

DAISY: (*Interrupting.*) Oh, please don't. I found what you said very moving.

EXTERMINATOR: Thank you.

DAISY: Almost familiar.

EXTERMINATOR: Really?

DAISY: Yes. It rang a bell somewhere deep inside me. I...

EXTERMINATOR: (*Interrupting*) Yes?

DAISY: Odd, but when you spoke it seemed... It's so ridiculous.

(*She laughs.*)

EXTERMINATOR: Of course it is. Too much to drink, perhaps.

DAISY: There was a boy. A young man, really...

EXTERMINATOR: (*Interrupting.*) Don't dwell too strenuously on it. Memory is a kind of illness, you know. It has its own way of inhibiting progress.

DAISY: That phrase you used. There was something you said that seemed...
(*A beat. She looks carefully at him. He is sitting Downstage, facing the audience.*)
"Cultural...

EXTERMINATOR: Thuggishness."

DAISY: Yes.

EXTERMINATOR: What about it?

DAISY: I know that phrase.

EXTERMINATOR: Is that right?

DAISY: I remember where I heard it.

EXTERMINATOR: That's nice.

(*A beat. She speaks to his back.*)

DAISY: Louis?

EXTERMINATOR: Excuse me?

DAISY: It's you, isn't it?

EXTERMINATOR: I don't know what you mean.

DAISY: You don't know what I mean? Funny. That's not like you. You used to know exactly what I meant, even before I did.

EXTERMINATOR: A case of mistaken identity, I'm afraid. I'm not familiar...

DAISY: (*Interrupting.*) Please don't.

EXTERMINATOR: I'm only...

DAISY: (*Interrupting.*) You have no idea, so please do not...

EXTERMINATOR: (*Interrupting.*) It's important to...

DAISY: (*Interrupting.*) "Eradicate memory?" I know. I've heard you say that. "History is a kind of poison. History is a kind of straitjacket. We have to reinvent ourselves." Well, I tried. Aw-right. Believe me, I tried.

(*They both gradually shift to Brooklyn accents.*)

DAISY: When ya left I remembered what ya said. I remembered your speeches, even years later.

EXTERMINATOR: It was inevitable. You knew...

DAISY: (*Interrupting.*) You coulda come to me! You coulda tole me!

EXTERMINATOR: (*Interrupting.*) You don't understand.

DAISY: No? Then explain it to me. Tell me how it's about sacrifice for the communal good. Tell me about all your plans for...

EXTERMINATOR: (*Interrupting.*) We can't let personality...

DAISY: (*Interrupting.*) Personality!?

EXTERMINATOR: The ego, then. The "me" generation thing. What you're talkin' about is a personal connection that...

DAISY: (*Interrupting.*) Personal connection? I'm talkin' about passion!

EXTERMINATOR: Awright. Use that word if you wanna. A "passion" that corrupts. I'm talkin' about somethin' larger.

DAISY: (*Interrupting.*) Don't gimme that! I don't wanna hear that.

EXTERMINATOR: No. I wouldn't expect ya to.

DAISY: You wouldn't expect me to what? Do you remembah the boardwalk, Louis? You remember dose nights on the beach, huh? How ya came ta me? You came ta me, didn't ya? Ya wanted me den, didn't ya? Goddamn you... Goddamn you!

EXTERMINATOR: Look. Try ta...

DAISY: (*She breaks down crying.*) I loved you!

(*A beat.*)

EXTERMINATOR: (*Tenderly.*) Ah course ya did. And I loved you. You were da love ah my life. (*He goes to her and holds her.*) I'm sorry. It's awright. I been stupid, okay? I guess havin' ya so close to me again was jus' too much, ya know?

(*He sings to her tenderly.*)

EXTERMINATOR: "By de sea, by de sea, by de beautiful sea..."

DAISY & EXTERMINATOR: (*Singing together.*) "You 'n me, you 'n me, oh how happy we'll be."

(*They laugh.*)

DAISY: Then ya do remembah?

EXTERMINATOR: Yeah.

DAISY: How 'bout...

EXTERMINATOR: (*Interrupting.*)   Ah course.   (*He sings, like Louis Armstrong*) "When you're smilin', when you're smilin', de whole world smiles wit you."

DAISY: Oh, Louis. It's good ta hold ya. It feels so right. When ya left...

EXTERMINATOR: (*Interrupting tenderly.*) Shhhh.

DAISY: I just thought...

EXTERMINATOR: Shhhh.

(*He takes DAISY's hand and they dance closely while he gently sings "Bicycle Built for Two."*)

EXTERMINATOR: "Daisy, Daisy, give me your answer, do.
I'm half crazy, all for the love of you.
It won't be a stylish marriage, I can't afford a carriage.
But you'll look sweet, upon the seat,
Of a bicycle built for two."

(*As the song ends his hands slowly move to her neck and he strangles her.*)

(*LIGHTS SLOWLY FADE TO BLACK.*)

END OF ACT II, SCENE 1

ACT TWO

Scene 2

(AT RISE: As the lights fade on Scene 1, the lights come up on Stage Left. It is a few minutes earlier. Moonlight streams down on a marshy, swampy dump site. Barrels of toxic waste, some torn open, spill out their contents. The area is covered with debris, garbage, body parts. Dead cats and other dead animals are frozen in positions of terror.

A mist rises from the ground. Strange vegetation. Trees covered with fungus. A blinking red railroad light. HARRY kneels by a swamp. He is holding SAMANTHA's legs as they sink into the ooze. He is humming "Bicycle Built for Two" in harmony with the EXTERMINATOR. Rocking slightly. Laughing to himself. He begins to fall asleep while still holding the legs. BENJIE emerges Upstage. He is out of breath, shirtless and barefoot, still wearing the black yarmulke. He carries his knife. His face and upper body are bloody, covered with slashes. He is mumbling and grimacing, trying to contain himself. He watches HARRY for a few moments. He quietly moves towards him. He stops a few feet from him. He begins to quietly speak, like a little boy.)

BENJIE: Hello, daddy.

HARRY: *(Waking.)* Huh?

BENJIE: Hello, daddy. What ya doing?

HARRY: Oh, hello boy. *(HARRY tries to hide SAMAN-THA's legs.)* I was just doing a little work around the garden.

79

BENJIE: Are you planting something?

HARRY: Yes, I am. (HARRY tries to push SAMAN-THA's legs down into the muck.) I'm planting seeds for the spring harvest. (*He turns and sees BENJIE's face.*) What happened to your face, boy?

(*BENJIE reaches up, touches his face. Sees blood on his hand.*)

BENJIE: Oh. I must have cut myself...shaving. Yes. That's it. I was shaving vegetables in the garden and something slipped.

HARRY: Well, we should be getting back inside before...

BENJIE: (*Interrupting.*) Wait. Please, daddy. Please do wait your turn. (*He moves close to HARRY's face. Speaks gently to him.*) The lines are forming to the rear, you know. Now the lines cannot stop forming. But if you're good we can make a special allowance in your case.

(*BENJIE smiles. He begins to shift into different personalities as though playing a child's game. He bows obsequiously to HARRY.*)

BENJIE: "We're ready. Right this way, Mr. Harry."

(*He takes HARRY by the arm. HARRY tries to pull away.*)

HARRY: I don't think this is necessary, boy. You're tired.

BENJIE: I'm bleeding.

HARRY: (*Ignoring this.*) I think we should just...

BENJIE: (*Interrupting. Childlike.*) I'm bleeding, daddy.

HARRY: I know, boy.

BENJIE: (*Intensely.*) Do you swear to tell the whole truth, and nothing but the truth, so help you God?

HARRY: Benjie.

BENJIE: The witness will answer the question. Do you swear to tell the holy...?

HARRY: (*Interrupting.*) Alright. I do.

BENJIE: Good. Very good.

HARRY: I don't know what you want. I don't know what you're talking about! I've got to go. I've got...I've got an appointment. I've got to...

(*HARRY tries to leave. BENJIE stops him.*)

HARRY: It's not my fault! I had nothing to do with it!

BENJIE: (*British Accent*) I'm afraid that we have witnesses to the contrary, Mister Harold. We have eye witnesses to the contrary. Mister H. (*BENJIE speak likes an old woman.*) "I saw the whole thing..."

(*BENJIE looks around as the old woman, sees HARRY and points him out.*)

BENJIE: (*In the voice of an old woman.*) "That's him! That's the one! I saw him! I saw him! I did! He's the one. I remember him. He was the one who did it!" (*In the kind voice of a prosecutor.*) "Are you absolutely certain, madam? After all, these are very serious charges being brought before this tribunal, concerning events which happened a long time ago."

(*He becomes the old woman again. She leans forward, looks at HARRY, and speaks with quiet intensity.*)

BENJIE: "Some things you never, ever forget. Some things stay with you for a lifetime. Some memories, some memories you live with them and you carry them with you until you die. Some things you never forget."

HARRY: Alright. Yes. Something did happen. There was some kind of an incident. But I wasn't directly involved.

BENJIE: (*Interrupting.*) Wrong.

HARRY: I don't remember the details, but someone else...

BENJIE: (*Interrupting.*) Wrong!

(*HARRY begins to break down. He starts to grovel and whimper. BENJIE is faced away from him.*)

HARRY: Let me go. Please. You've got to understand I was just doing my assignment. Just what they told me to do. I swear to God I can't even remember what happened. It was such a long time ago. I'm sorry. I'm so sorry.

BENJIE: (*Quietly. Not looking at HARRY.*) You're asking for...leniency, then?

HARRY: Yes. Extenuating circumstances. It was a terrible mistake. I'll admit that to you right now. An error of judgment. You're absolutely right about that. A terrible, terrible accident. (*BENJIE is still looking away.*) But I'll make it up to you. Give me a chance to make it up to you. Will you do that? Will you?

(*A beat. BENJIE is lost in thought.*)

BENJIE: (*Looks upward as if listening to someone. Quietly.*) Yes. Nobody's fault. An act of God.

HARRY: That's it! An act of God. That's it, exactly. I had no choice. They told me. They told me what to do. (*A beat. Like a little boy.*) I was scared. I was scared they would hurt me. (*He crawls to BENJIE and hugs his legs.*) I'm weak. I'm a weak old man. Please, boy. They made me.

(*BENJIE turns slowly and looks at HARRY.*)

BENJIE: (*Softly.*) They made you? They made you do it?

HARRY: Yes.

(*BENJIE looks upward. His eyes light up. He smiles. He turns slowly to HARRY.*)

BENJIE: (*Softly.*) Me, too.

(*BENJIE quickly cuts HARRY's throat. As HARRY dies, BENJIE continues to rock him. He sings the song that HARRY had earlier sung to the EXTERMINATOR.*)

BENJIE: "Yie yieyieyieyieyie....."

(*He stops singing abruptly. He sniffs the air like an ani-*

mal and looks back towards the house. He carefully lays HARRY down on the ground. He kneels. He lifts HARRY's hand and places it on his own head like a bene-diction. He lays the hand down. A beat. Then he moves on all fours into the woods and towards the house. LIGHTS FADE.)

END OF ACT TWO, SCENE 2

ACT TWO

Scene 3

(AT RISE: We're back in the house. It's a few moments later. DAISY's body lies on the living room floor. BENJIE emerges on all fours from the kitchen entrance. He stealthily crawls to the living room. He is sniffing and looking around. He sees DAISY. He freezes momentarily. He crawls over. He sniffs her. Nuzzles her. Licks her face. Nuzzles her again. Suddenly he hears something. Freezes and looks up abruptly. He quickly and silently crawls behind the Stage Right sofa. He waits expectantly. The EXTERMINATOR emerges from the upstairs bedroom. He is again wearing his full bodysuit and gear. He is exterminating the house. He is shooting occasional vapors from his gun. Suddenly he pauses, as if he senses that something is wrong. He sniffs the air. Slowly and carefully, he begins to make his way forward, cautiously looking around. As the EXTERMINATOR cautiously moves forward, BENJIE begins to make cat sounds.)

BENJIE: *(Very quietly.)* Meow. Meow.

(When he hears this, the EXTERMINATOR freezes. There is a moment of silence.)

BENJIE: Meee-ow. Meee-ow.

(Now, the EXTERMINATOR continues warily into the living room.)

EXTERMINATOR: *(Gently.)* Here, kitty. Here, kitty kitty...

BENJIE: Meee-ow!

EXTERMINATOR: Here, kitty.

(*BENJIE crouches behind the couch, holding his knife, ready to spring. The EXTERMINATOR moves warily towards the couch with his vapor gun ready. They speak simultaneously.*)

BENJIE: Mee-ow. Meee-ow. Meee-ow. Mee-ow.
    Meeow.

EXTERMINATOR: Heeere, kitty. Here kitty. Here
    kitty, kitty. Here kitty, kitty.

(*Slow fade to black.*)

THE PLAY ENDS.

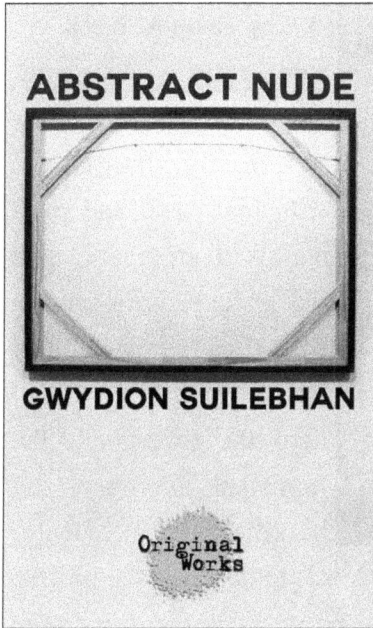

ABSTRACT NUDE

GWYDION SUILEBHAN

Original
Works

Abstract Nude

by Gwydion Suilebhan

Synopsis: "Abstract Nude" is an enigmatic, erotically-charged portrait that seems to reveal more about the people who view it than it reveals about itself. As the painting moves backward in time, it passes from owner to owner, exploding the lives of everyone who encounters it. In one home, the portrait tips the balance in a barely-suppressed power struggle among the members of a well-to-do family. In another, it awakens a great deal of confusion – and passion – between two former fraternity brothers. In the home of the portrait's subject, it inspires nothing but unrequited love and alienation between two dear friends. And finally, back in the moment of its creation, where the story both ends and begins, the painting incites a terrible violence… the tragedy that haunts it wherever it travels, and that cannot be escaped.

Cast Size: 4 Males, 3 Females

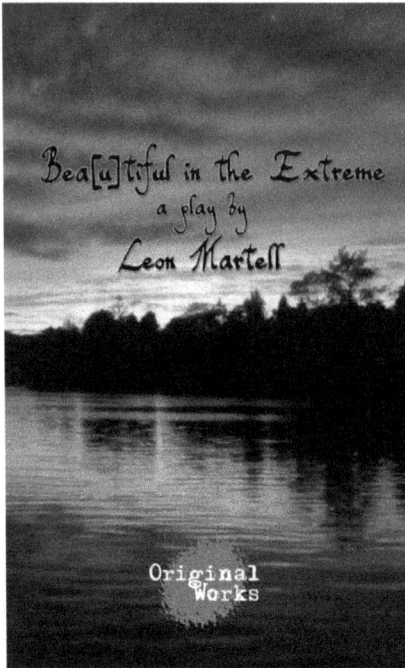

Bea[u]tiful in the Extreme
by Leon Martell

Synopsis: America, 1809. Barely in his thirties, Meriwether Lewis, with his friend and partner William Clark, had led an expedition across the continent and back. He was a national hero, the governor of the Louisiana Territory, and he killed himself. Bea[u]tiful in the Extreme, his own words to describe the prairie, follows Meriwether Lewis as he wrestles the demons in his mind. Between the time of his first suicide attempt on a flat boat down the Mississippi, and his final self execution in an inn on the Natchez trace, Lewis relives the triumphs and trials of his epic journey. With Thomas Jefferson, his mentor, Sacagawea the native girl as his guide, and William Clark, his friend, anchor and in many ways soul mate, he struggles to find meaning in all he has seen and done. A warrior faces evil spirits, broken dreams, and politicians in his final battle. Whiskey, meat, laughs, and laudanum on the long trail to immortality.

Cast Size: 9 or more actors playing multiple roles

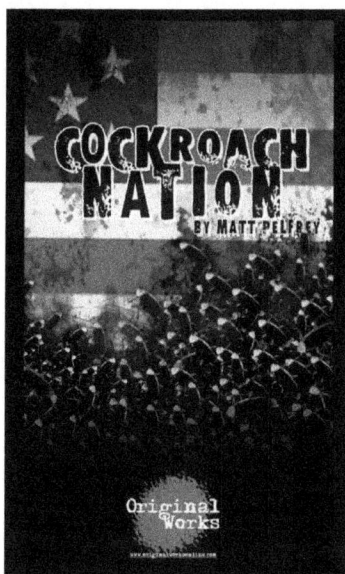

<u>Cockroach Nation</u> by Matt Pelfrey

Synopsis: A yuppie ad-exec, Hank, finds himself lost in a dark alley where he undergoes a transformation to homelessness and insanity. He is in the longest, dirtiest alley in the city where he meets the resident of the underbelly of a world that is rocketing towards chaos. There's Boone, a self-styled leader who has adopted guerilla warfare tactics to survive in this world. His sidekick Cockroach Boy is an eerie Kafkaesque part roach like humanoid scampers on all fours, and talks in clicks, hisses, whistles and grunts. And the Trash King, a mythic being who spouts philosophical observations warning that trash will outlive us all. "The wrapper outlasts the burger - the bottle outlasts the wine - the can outlasts the Coke..."

Cast Size: 8 Males, 4 Females

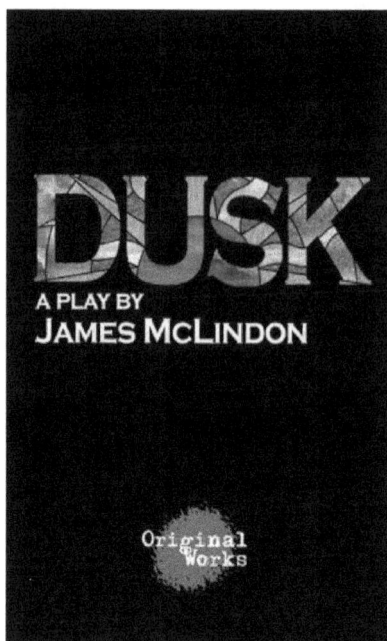

<u>Dusk</u> by James McLindon

Synopsis: Dusk is that time of day when, "if you didn't know what time it was, you wouldn't know which is going to win, the light or the darkness." So says Nana, the matriarch of an Irish Catholic family in Cambridge, Massachusetts struggling to decide whether to accept the Church's settlement offer or go to trial over a priest's sexual assault of the family's youngest son. Over the course of one day, the family must face truth and lies, faith and disillusionment; and betrayal, forgiveness, and redemption on their journey toward peace.

Cast Size: 2 Males, 2 Females

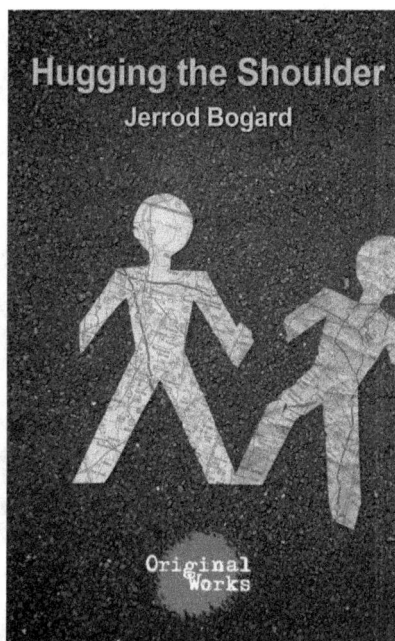

Hugging The Shoulder by Jerrod Bogard

Synopsis: A young man kidnaps his big brother, locks him in a van, and drives him across the country in an attempt to get him off heroin. Mile after mile, their relationship is put to the test, and little brother must decide how far he is willing to go. Hugging the Shoulder asks the question; Am I my brother's keeper?

Cast Size: 2 Males, 1 Female, 1 Either

The Princeton Seventh by James Vculek

Synopsis: Two strangers start up a contentious conversation in a bar while they wait for a tribute to a dead poet. From that inauspicious beginning, the layers start to fall away and the twists start to pile up. When they are joined by a Nobel Prize winning author and his current trophy wife, the entanglements and revelations multiply. The play ends and then... it begins again. Or does it?

Cast Size: 3 Males, 2 Females

owl moon

a play by Liz Maestri

Original
Works

Owl Moon
by Liz Maestri

Synopsis: What happens when an Owl Moon rises? The everyday world veers into extremities – hot blood spurts and passions seep into a wintry landscape of cold and desolation. Two couples venture into a desolate, frozen snowfield for the night where they find themselves trapped, both physically and in the mire of their own neurosis. Lisa is determined to win back her ex, Isaac, and will stop at nothing to do so. Shell and Salome carry weighty sacks across the snow, looking for a way to purge their sins. The play follows this group of characters through conflicts and collisions that stretch taut conventions of style and tone. Is it possible to lose oneself? To lose oneself in another? Owl Moon examines the fine line between passion and obsession, and the toll it takes on the mind and spirit. Add in a talking owl, and you have a play that juggles the heady, humorous and harrowing in equal measure.

Cast Size: 1 Male, 3 Females, 1 Talking Owl

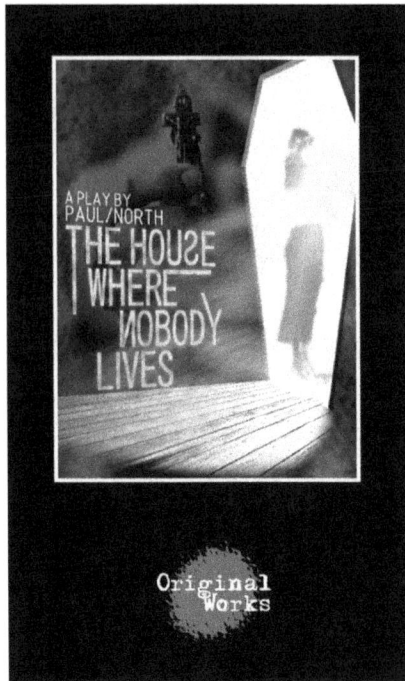

The House Where Nobody Lives by Paul North

Synopsis: A man who thinks he's at sea, a woman who believes that she's in a library, a heroin addict, and an orphan make a difficult task for Sarah, the woman assigned to maintain their illusions. When these illusions begin to collide, moments of comedy and chaos erupt, and we watch Sarah try to retain order, but the House gives no second chances.

Cast Size: 3 Males, 2 Females

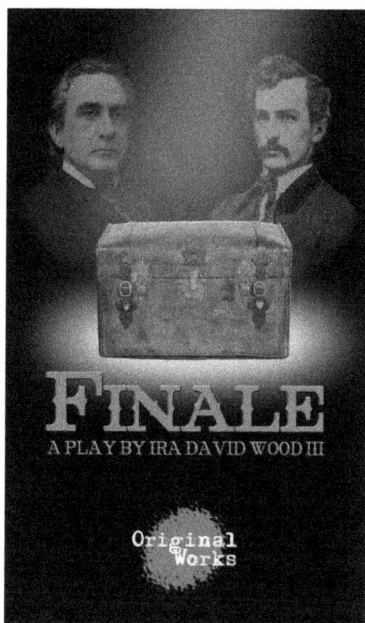

FINALE

A PLAY BY IRA DAVID WOOD III

Original Works

Finale by **Ira David Wood III**

Synopsis: A haunting tale of family, history, regrets and shame. The Booth family was America's greatest acting clan. Generations of Booth sons tread the boards of American stages garnering great acclaim and riches until the youngest and arguably most famous of them all, John Wilkes, turned the country upside down. Eight years after the assassination of President Lincoln, Edwin Booth returns to his family's theatre in New York to sort through his younger brother's storage trunk which the government has recently returned. Ghostly memories of his father and brother appear to him as he struggles to rectify issues that have plagued his family name since that fateful night at Ford's Theater.

Cast Size: 5 Males, 3 Females

NOTES

NOTES

NOTES

NOTES

www.ingramcontent.com/pod-product-compliance
Lightning Source LLC
Chambersburg PA
CBHW062010040426
42447CB00010B/1986